MATERIALS AND PROCESSES

Peter Riley

FRANKLIN WATTS
A Division of Grolier Publishing
NEW YORK • LONDON • HONG KONG • SYDNEY
DANBURY, CONNECTICUT

© Franklin Watts 1998
Text © Peter Riley 1998

First American Edition 1998 by
Franklin Watts
Grolier Publishing Co., Inc.
90 Sherman Turnpike
Danbury, CT 06816

Visit Franklin Watts
on the Internet at:
http://publishing.grolier.com

Editor: Sarah Snashall
Art director: Robert Walster
Designer: Mo Choy
Picture research: Sue Mennell
Photography: Steve Shott (unless
otherwise credited)
Artwork: Sean Wilkinson

Printed in Belgium

Library of Congress Cataloging-in-
Publication Data
Riley, Peter D.
Materials and processes / Peter Riley
p.   cm. -- (Straightforward Science)
Includes index
   Summary: Text and activities
demonstrate that materials are solids,
liquids, or gases and while they have
special distinguishing features called
properties, they can be changed in
ways known as processes.
ISBN: 0-531-11514-3 (lib. bdg.)
       0-531-15369-X (pbk.)
   1. Materials --Study and teaching--
Activity programs-Juvenile literature.
[1. Materials.]   I. Title   II. Series:
Riley, Peter D.   Straightforward
Science.
TA403.2.R56   1997
530--dc21   97-45602CIP
AC

Picture credits:
Robert Harding p.22m
(Martyn F. Chillmaid)
The Image Bank p.19l
(Nick Pavloff)
Images Colour Library pp. 9b, 17tl,
17tr, 18t, 20 (both), 21tm,
21tr, 27l
Life Science Images p.25t
Ray Muller pp. 2, 19r
Science Photo Library pp. 9t,
24b (Adrienne Hart-Davis), 28b
(P. Nieto, Jerrican), 29l (ITAR-
TASS/European Space Agency), 29r
(Dr. Jeremy Burgess)
Still Pictures p.23t
(Andre Maslennikov),
20tl (Marc Rapillard)
The Stockmarket p. 11b
Tony Stone Images p.5t
(Pal Hermansen)
Telegraph Colour Library p. 28t

CONTENTS

⧗ MATERIALS AROUND US

There are thousands of different materials. They are all around you. Clothes are made of wool, cotton, and nylon. Homes are made of brick, wood, and glass. The earth is made of rock, and the surface of the land is covered with soil and water. Every one of these things — wool, cotton, nylon, brick, wood, glass, rock, soil, and water — is a material.

Steel is magnetic. It is attracted to a magnet.

Pottery is brittle. It breaks if it is struck hard.

Cloth is absorbent. It soaks up water.

Plastic is lightweight. It has a small weight for its size.

Water is a solvent. Other substances dissolve in it.

Glass is transparent. Light can pass straight through it.

Stone is heavy. It has a large weight for its size.

Paper is flexible. It bends easily.

PROPERTIES

Materials have properties. A property is a special feature of a material. One property of wood is that it is hard. One property of wool is that it is soft. A material can have other properties. It may be strong or weak, flexible or rigid, magnetic or nonmagnetic, transparent or opaque.

Wood is flexible. The branches of a tree can bend in the wind.

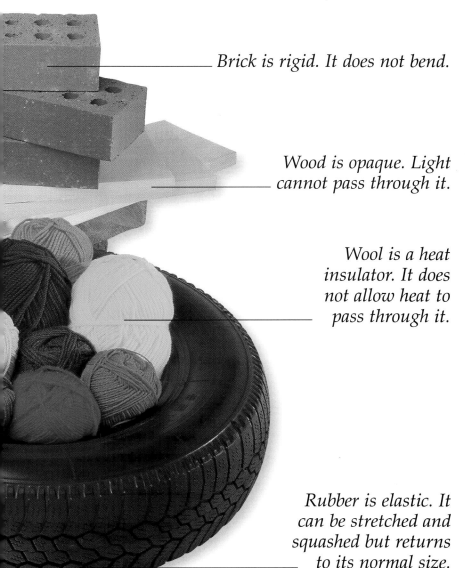

Brick is rigid. It does not bend.

Wood is opaque. Light cannot pass through it.

Wool is a heat insulator. It does not allow heat to pass through it.

Rubber is elastic. It can be stretched and squashed but returns to its normal size.

The nail does not break when the hammer hits it because it is not brittle. What would happen if the hammer hit the glass?

■ INVESTIGATE!

List the properties of the materials that make up a window and frame. What materials could have been used instead?

USING MATERIALS

We choose materials to use because they have certain properties. Cotton is soft, and this makes it useful for clothing. Glass is transparent, and this makes it useful for making windows.

LOTS OF PROPERTIES

Usually it is not just one property of a material that makes it useful, but the combination of its properties. Wood is strong, hard, and light in weight.

Each of these properties is useful for making a chair. When you sit on a wooden chair, the wood's strength supports your weight and stops the chair from bending. The wood is light enough for you to move it easily. Its surface is hard and not easily chipped if it is accidentally knocked by a shoe.

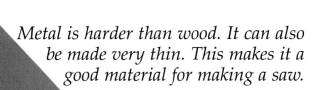

Metal is harder than wood. It can also be made very thin. This makes it a good material for making a saw.

Rubber is elastic and durable, and it grips the road. This makes it suitable for making car tires.

COMBINING MATERIALS

Many things we use need to have a number of properties. Sneakers have to be lightweight, durable, springy, firm, and absorbent. No single material has all these properties, so a combination of materials is used to make the shoes.

The feet are covered in a moisture-absorbing fabric.

The top of the shoes is made from a fabric that allows moisture to pass through it.

The soles are made from rubber, which is flexible and durable. The rubber and fabric are held together with strong glue.

INVESTIGATE!

What are the useful properties of cloth in a curtain, rubber in a bicycle tire, and metal in a pair of scissors?

Conducting Heat

Some materials let heat travel through them. They are called conductors of heat. Materials that do not let heat travel through them are called insulators.

Metals and Pots

Metals are good conductors of heat. Pots are made of metal because the metal lets heat from the stove pass quickly to the food and cook it.

Central Heating

Radiators in a central heating system are made of metal. Hot water moves from the boiler through the pipes to the radiators. The heat in the water passes quickly through the metal in the radiators and out into the air to heat the room.

These clothes are being dried on a central heating radiator because the metal passes heat quickly to them.

STOPPING HEAT MOVEMENT

Some plastics are heat insulators. They are used to make the handles of pots and kettles. The surface of the plastic handle stays cool to hold even though the pot or kettle is very hot. Wood is also a heat insulator. Some pot handles are made of wood.

KEEPING WARM

Air is an insulator. Some materials trap air inside them. The air turns the material into an insulator too. Wool fibers are wavy and have air spaces between them. A woolen sweater traps a layer of air against your skin. It stops your body heat from escaping and keeps you warm.

The air spaces between the woolen fibers stop heat from traveling through the material.

▌INVESTIGATE!

Fill two plastic cups with warm water, and wrap a piece of cotton cloth around one cup and a piece of woolen cloth around the other. Which cup of water stays warm longer? Which material is the better insulator?

This climber is wearing a number of heat-insulating layers to keep warm in the cold wind. Air is trapped between each layer.

CONDUCTING ELECTRICITY

Many things we use in today's world need electricity to work. The electricity flows from a source of electricity to an appliance through a wire. The wire is a conductor of electricity. It lets the current of electricity flow through it. Most materials do not let electricity flow through them. They are called electrical insulators.

CONDUCTORS

Metals such as iron, steel, copper, and aluminum are electrical conductors. The black material called graphite in a pencil is not a metal, but it conducts electricity. Water also conducts electricity.

INSULATORS

Wood, paper, plastic, bricks, and pottery are insulators. Air is an insulator too. If it was a conductor, the bulb would light even when there was a gap in the circuit.

In the circuit above, the lightbulb is on because the metal spoon in the circuit is an electrical conductor. It would not go on if the spoon were made of wood. A circuit like this one can be used to test materials to find out if they are electrical conductors or electrical insulators.

Touching an electric current can kill you. Great care must be taken when handling any electrical equipment.

CONDUCTORS AND INSULATORS IN USE

Conductors and insulators are used to send electricity safely from one place to another. Electricity is conducted from plug sockets to appliances by copper wires coated in plastic. The metal takes the electricity along the wire, and the plastic coating stops the electricity from leaving through the sides when the wire touches other objects.

Plugs, cords, and switches are all covered in plastic to stop the electricity in the metal from reaching your fingers.

INVESTIGATE!

Set up the circuit shown on page 10. Test different materials to find out which are conductors and which are insulators.

Electricity is conducted from power stations along metal cables that are held on metal towers. Insulating material between the cables and the towers stops the electricity flowing down the towers to the ground.

MATERIALS AT HOME

Every house is made from a large number of materials. Each material has special properties and is used for a particular task. The different materials are used together to make a house.

Plastic is lightweight and easily shaped. It is used to make gutters and pipes that carry water to the drains.

Bricks are strong and do not break up in the rain, wind, and frost. They make weather-resistant walls that can support the weight of the roof.

Cement holds the bricks together like glue.

Glass is weather-resistant and transparent. It lets light into the home but keeps out the wind and the rain.

Paint is a mixture of a colored powder and a liquid. Paint forms a protective coating on wood and stops it from soaking up water and rotting.

Roof shingles are made of baked clay and are weather-resistant.

Rock wool forms a thick insulation blanket that traps air and stops heat from escaping through the roof.

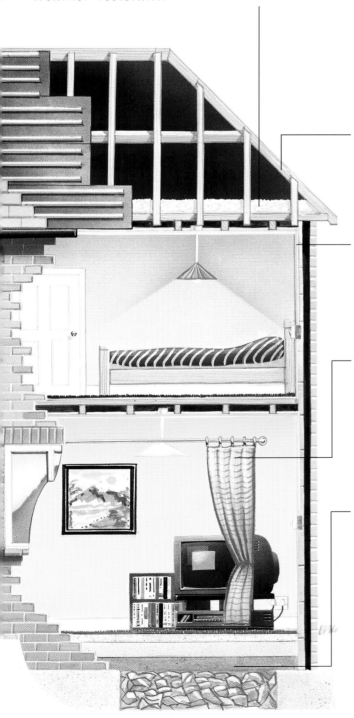

Wood is strong yet light in weight and easily shaped. It is used to make the window frames and doors and the roof supports that rest on the walls and hold the roof shingles.

Electricity is brought to the home by metal cables covered in a coat of insulating material.

Lightweight, opaque fabrics are used to make curtains, and heavier, durable fabrics are used to make carpets and furniture coverings.

Concrete is very strong and durable. It is used to make the foundations on which the house is built. It may also be used for the ground floor and for the paths outside.

■ INVESTIGATE!

Scratch some discarded pieces of wood, brick, concrete, and plastic. Which material has the hardest surface?

SOLIDS, LIQUIDS, AND GASES

Most of the materials around us are solid materials. There are two other types of materials. They are liquids and gases. All materials can be put into one of these three groups: solids, liquids, or gases. The materials in each group have properties that are different from the materials in the other two groups.

A SOLID

A solid material has a definite shape and a definite size or volume. It cannot be squashed to fit into a smaller space. Tiny pieces of solids can flow together like the sand in an egg timer, but they do not form drops. Most of the materials around us are solids.

Some solids, like these minerals, have a crystal shape.

A LIQUID

A liquid does not have a definite shape. It can flow and take up the shape of any container into which it is poured. It also forms drops. A liquid has a definite volume, which stays the same even if you try to squash it.

Water is the most common liquid, but oil and syrup are liquids too.

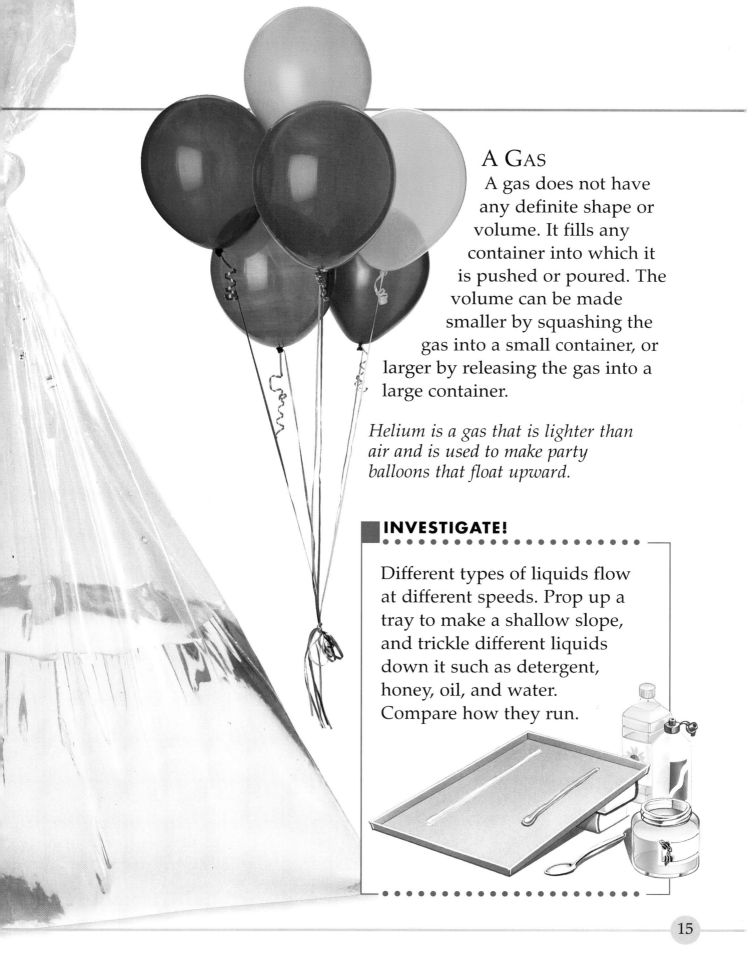

A GAS

A gas does not have any definite shape or volume. It fills any container into which it is pushed or poured. The volume can be made smaller by squashing the gas into a small container, or larger by releasing the gas into a large container.

Helium is a gas that is lighter than air and is used to make party balloons that float upward.

■ INVESTIGATE!

Different types of liquids flow at different speeds. Prop up a tray to make a shallow slope, and trickle different liquids down it such as detergent, honey, oil, and water. Compare how they run.

SOLID TO LIQUID

Many solid materials turn into a liquid when they are heated enough. If they are left to cool down, they turn back into solids again.

HEATING UP
When a solid loses its shape and turns into a liquid, we say it has melted. The temperature at which a solid melts is called its melting point. The melting point of ice is 32°F (0°C). Solids have different melting points. The melting point of chocolate is 91°F (33°C). The melting point of aluminum is 1221°F (660.5°C).

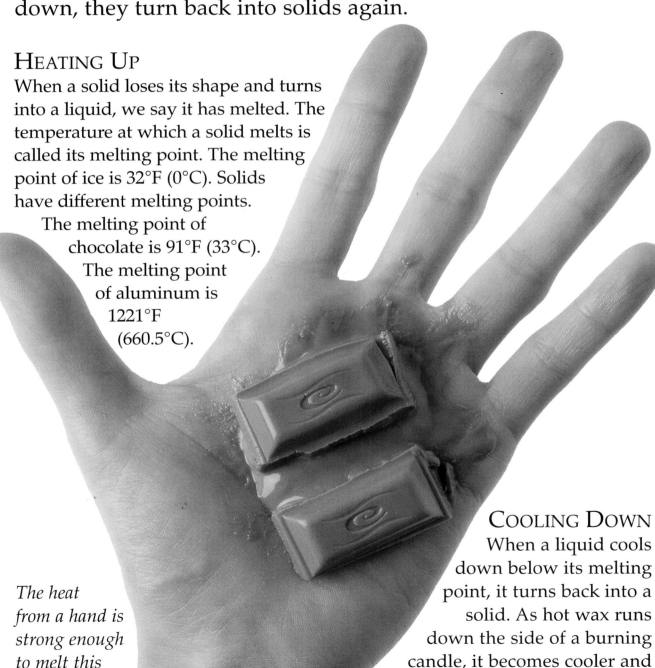

The heat from a hand is strong enough to melt this chocolate.

COOLING DOWN
When a liquid cools down below its melting point, it turns back into a solid. As hot wax runs down the side of a burning candle, it becomes cooler and turns back into a solid.

These icicles are dripping because the weather is warm enough to melt them.

The water on this window has frozen into "fern frost."

FREEZING

When liquid materials are cooled down, they turn into a solid. If they are left to warm up, they turn back into a liquid. The point at which they turn into a solid is called the freezing point. The freezing point of water is 32°F (0°C). At 32°F (0°C), water turns into ice.

REVERSIBLE CHANGES

When water freezes and becomes ice, it is easy to turn it back into a liquid again by melting it. Freezing is a reversible change — in other words, it can be undone. Reversible changes are arranged in pairs. One of the changes is the opposite of the other. The opposite of freezing is melting.

■ INVESTIGATE!

Half fill a plastic bottle with water. Draw a line to mark the level of the water. Leave the bottle in the freezer until the water has frozen. What happens to the water level?

LIQUID TO GAS

A liquid can turn into a gas by evaporating or by boiling.

EVAPORATION

When water is left uncovered, the water slowly changes into a gas and mixes with the air. This is called evaporation. The gas formed when water evaporates is called water vapor. Wet clothes dry by evaporation when they are hung on a line.

Nearly three-quarters of the earth is covered by water. Evaporation takes place at its surface, and the invisible water vapor mixes with the air.

BOILING

When a liquid is heated enough, some of it turns to gas and forms bubbles. They rise to the surface of the liquid and escape into the air. A hot bubbling liquid is called a boiling liquid. The temperature at which a liquid boils is called its boiling point. The boiling point of water is 212°F (100°C).

Bubbles of steam rise through the boiling water.

CONDENSATION

Gases change into liquids by condensation. Water vapor is in the air all the time. It condenses when it comes in contact with cold surfaces, like the inside of a window on a cold day. When steam mixes with air, it cools below 212°F (100°C) and turns into clouds of tiny water droplets.

——————Water droplets

Steam ——————

As steam is cooled down by the air, it turns into a cloud of water droplets.

When the air is cold above the surface of the ground, water vapor condenses on the grass and forms dew.

MORE REVERSIBLE CHANGES

Evaporation and condensation are reversible changes. A liquid changes into a gas by evaporation, and a gas changes back into a liquid by condensation. Boiling and condensation are reversible changes too.

▌ INVESTIGATE!

Take a cold object such as a canned drink from a refrigerator and breathe on it. Look for water condensing on the object.

THE WATER CYCLE

Water travels in a circular path. Water evaporates from the surface of seas and oceans; it travels through the air and through the soil and plants. It falls as rain and returns to the seas and oceans. This path is called the water cycle.

EVAPORATION AND CONDENSATION

At the surface of every ocean, sea, and lake, water evaporates into the air and forms water vapor. It spreads out through the air. The air is full of tiny particles of dust. High in the air these dust particles are cold. When water vapor reaches them, it condenses on their surfaces and forms tiny water droplets. Billions of droplets form at once and make a cloud. The wind blow the clouds away.

FREEZING

When the clouds are blown into a colder region, such as over a hilltop, the droplets at the top of the cloud freeze. They turn to ice crystals, which join together and form snowflakes.

The air lower in the cloud is warmer than the air at the top. As the snowflakes fall through the cloud, they melt and turn into large drops of water. The clouds look dark and threatening.

RAIN

The large drops are too heavy to stay in the cloud, so they fall as rain.

OVER THE GROUND

The rainwater flows away in streams and rivers back to the lakes and seas.

FROM THE GROUND TO THE AIR

Rainwater soaks into the soil and is taken up by plant roots. Most of the water passes through the plant and escapes through the leaves as water vapor.

A diagram of the water cycle.
1. The water evaporates. 2. Clouds form. 3. The water in the clouds freezes. 4. The water falls as rain. 5. Plants soak up the rainwater. 6. Rainwater flows back to the sea. The process begins again.

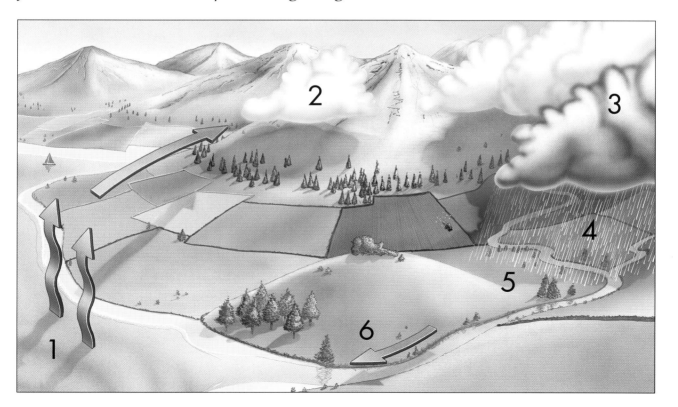

MIXING

Different materials can be mixed together. The mixture formed may have different properties from those of the materials it is made from.

MIXING SOLIDS AND LIQUIDS

Dry clay is made from tiny particles that you can see. Water is made from very tiny particles you cannot see. When the clay and water are mixed, the clay particles separate and spread out between the water particles. The two materials form a new material that can hold a shape.

This clay and water mixture is being shaped into a vase.

DISSOLVING

Sugar and salt are materials that dissolve in water. When a material dissolves, it splits up into very tiny particles you cannot see. The particles spread out between the water particles and make the salt or sugar seem to disappear.

The sugar in this spoon dissolves as soon as it touches the water.

THE AIR WE BREATHE

Air is a mixture of gases. One of the gases in the mixture is oxygen. We take this gas from the air when we breathe in and use it to stay alive.

Gases from car engines mix with the air. Some of these gases are harmful. If they occur in large amounts in the air, they cause air pollution, which can damage people's health.

When car and truck engines are working, they burn fuel and make gases that pass down an exhaust pipe and into the air.

MATERIALS THAT DON'T MIX

Some materials appear to mix at first but separate later. When particles of soil are mixed with water in a jar, they form a cloudy suspension. This means that the soil particles are just hanging in the water. In time, the particles settle to the bottom of the jar and form a sediment.

The suspension of soil in the water (left) soon settles out into a sediment at the bottom of the jar (right).

■ INVESTIGATE!

Stir some oil and water together. Can you get them to mix?

SEPARATING MATERIALS

Some materials that have been mixed together can be separated again later. Sieving and filtering can be used to separate particles of different sizes. Evaporating can be used to separate water from the materials dissolved in it.

SIEVING

A sieve can be used to separate a mixture of two solid materials that have particles of different sizes. There are holes in a sieve. Material particles that are larger than the holes stay in the sieve. Material particles that are smaller than the holes pass through the sieve.

FILTERING

A mixture of a liquid and a solid that does not dissolve can be separated using a very fine sieve called a filter. Most filters are made of paper that has tiny holes in it. The liquid can squeeze through the holes, but the solid cannot.

The filter that this cyclist is wearing separates the dust from the mixture of air and dust he is breathing.

EVAPORATION

A liquid and a solid can be separated by evaporation. If the mixture is poured into a dish, the water evaporates. When it does this, the water particles escape into the air and form water vapor. The solid particles cannot do this and are left behind in the dish.

DISTILLATION

Ink is a mixture of water and dissolved color particles. They can be separated by heating and cooling. The ink is heated in the flask and the water turns to steam. The steam passes along the pipe and cools down. It condenses to water in the pipe and drips out into the beaker.

▇ INVESTIGATE!
• • • • • • • • • • • • • • •

Sieve some whole wheat flour to make some white flour.

• • • • • • • • • • • • • •

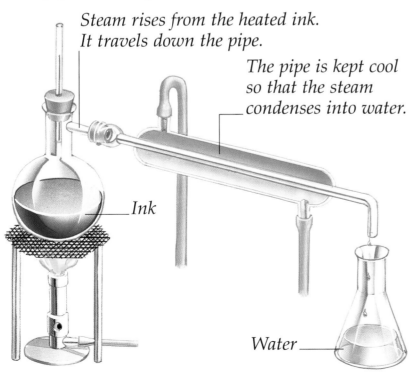

Steam rises from the heated ink. It travels down the pipe.

The pipe is kept cool so that the steam condenses into water.

Ink

Water

REVERSIBLE CHANGES

Separating materials is the opposite, or the reverse, of mixing them. Separating is a reversible change. Mixing is sometimes a reversible change.

PERMANENT CHANGES

Some processes cannot be reversed. They are called nonreversible, or permanent, changes. Some mixtures are nonreversible. Nonreversible changes can take place when materials and mixtures are heated.

BAKING BREAD
Some bread is made from flour, water, yeast, and sugar. These four ingredients are mixed together to make dough. Yeast is a type of fungus. It feeds on sugar.

The ingredients for making bread.

This lump of dough is warming in a bread pan while the yeast feeds. After baking, it will become a loaf.

When the dough is warmed, the yeast feeds quickly and grows. As it feeds, the yeast makes carbon dioxide gas. This forms bubbles in the dough and makes it rise. When the dough is baked, the yeast is destroyed, the flour is made digestible, and the bubbles in the dough expand and make it spongy. The change from dough to bread cannot be reversed.

BURNING

When some materials get hot, they burst into flame and burn. They produce the gas carbon dioxide, which escapes into the air. A material called ash is left behind. The black color in ash is carbon that has not changed to carbon dioxide. The rest of the ash is made from other substances that were in the material. Burning is a nonreversible reaction.

Ash is left behind as wood burns on an open fire.

FIRING

When clay is heated to extreme temperatures, its particles stick together to make a hard, brittle material that is used for pottery and bricks. This process is called firing.

▉ INVESTIGATE!

Examine some food before it is cooked, and make notes about its properties. Examine the food after it has been cooked. Discover how its properties have changed.

NEW MATERIALS

The world is full of natural materials such as wood and stone that we can use. By mixing and heating natural materials, we can make new materials with new properties.

Liquid steel is poured into a mold, which shapes the metal as it cools down.

MIXING METALS

Iron is a natural metal. It is strong but brittle. If iron is melted and oxygen is blown through the liquid iron, steel is made. Steel is also strong, but not brittle. Steel is used to make wire, cans, and car bodies. Steel rusts when it gets damp. If it is mixed with the metals nickel and chromium, stainless steel is made, which does not rust. It can be used to make kitchen sinks and cutlery.

The steel in these scrapped cars is about to be recycled. It may be made into scissors or paper clips next time.

Lightweight and heat-resistant materials are needed to build rockets for spacecraft.

KEEPING DRY

Many scientists work to develop new materials. The materials have properties that are helpful in special ways. Gore-Tex is an example of a new material that allows sweat to escape from a jacket without rainwater soaking in.
It allows people to feel more comfortable when they are hiking or climbing.

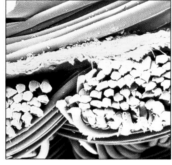

This is a close-up picture of the fabric Gore-Tex, which is made from a combination of materials.

MATERIALS IN SPACE

New materials have allowed us to explore space. Cermets are materials made from metals and ceramics. They do not break up when they get very hot and are used in making rockets.

INVESTIGATE!

Make lists of the natural and manufactured materials you use. Which list is longer?

GLOSSARY

ABSORBENT – a property of a solid material that has tiny spaces in it. The solid can take up a liquid into the spaces. Some solids can also take up gases and are used to remove smells, such as that of sweaty feet in shoes.

ASH – a gray-black powder that is a mixture of substances from a material that has been burned.

BOILER – a metal tank that is kept full of water and is heated to provide hot water for a home.

CEMENT – a substance used to stick bricks together. It is made from clay and limestone that have been heated together, then made into a powder and mixed with water.

CERAMIC – a material made of baked clay.

COMBINATION – a group of things put together. A material can have a combination of properties. This means it has a number of different properties. An object can be made from a combination of materials.

This means it is made from a number of different materials combined together.

CONCRETE – a hard substance made by mixing sand, cement, small pieces of rock, and water together and used for making paths, foundations to houses, and the supports in tall buildings and bridges.

CONDUCTOR – a material, such as a metal, that electricity or heat can pass though.

CORDS – wires coated with plastic that are used to carry electricity. A cord usually has a plug at both ends. One end is plugged into a piece of equipment and the other end into a supply of electricity.

CRYSTAL – a solid material with flat sides arranged at angles to each other. Table salt is a common crystal.

DISTILLATION – a process of separating a solid and a liquid by heating and cooling. The

solid is dissolved in the liquid and makes a solution. This is heated and the liquid turns into a gas, leaving the dissolved substance behind as a solid. The gas is then cooled away from the solid and turns back into a liquid.

FABRIC – a material made from threads of wool, cotton, nylon, or other kinds of fibers. The threads are woven or knitted together to make a piece of cloth.

FILTER – a material such as paper or cloth that is used to separate very small solid particles from liquids and gases.

FLEXIBLE – a property of a material that allows it to be bent without breaking.

FROST – water vapor that has condensed on the ground or on windows, then has frozen.

GLASS – a hard, brittle, usually transparent substance that is made by heating sand at high temperatures with limestone and a chemical called soda.

ICICLE – a long, thin, pointed piece of ice that hangs down usually from a roof. It forms when dripping water freezes.

INSULATOR – a material such as thick wool that does not let heat pass through it, or a material such as pottery or wood that does not let electricity pass through it.

OPAQUE – a property of a material such as stone that prevents it from letting light pass through it.

RADIATOR – a piece of equipment that gives off heat to warm up a room. It may be filled with water, which moves through pipes to a boiler. The hot water comes from the boiler to the radiator, and the water's heat is lost into the air.

RECYCLE – a process in which a material such as metal, glass, or plastic is used again. The process begins by separating the material from trash, then sending it to a factory where it is cleaned, heated, and made into a new object.

RIGID – a property of a material that prevents the material from being bent or squashed or stretched. The material keeps its shape when it is pushed and pulled by strong forces.

ROCKET – a type of engine on a spacecraft . Fuel is burned in it to produce a force that moves the spacecraft. Large rocket engines are used to launch spacecraft from the earth. Small rocket engines on spacecraft are used to steer spacecraft in space.

ROCK WOOL – a material made from fine fibers. The fibers are made by blowing steam through molten rock.

SEDIMENT – a layer of solid particles that forms at the bottom of a container holding a liquid. The particles do not dissolve in the liquid. They sink to the bottom of the container.

SIEVE – a piece of equipment with holes in it or made from wire netting. It is used for separating solid particles of different sizes such as sand and small stones.

SOLVENT – a liquid that can dissolve other substances in it. Water is a solvent. It can dissolve solids such as sugar and gases such as carbon dioxide to make soda.

STEEL – a metal made from iron. There are different kinds of steel. They are used for making food cans, car bodies, girders, and saws.

SYRUP – a liquid made by dissolving sugar in boiling water. It is used to make candy.

TEMPERATURE – a measure of the hotness or coldness of a substance. It is measured by using a scale on a thermometer.

TRANSPARENT – a property of a material such as glass or water that lets light pass through it.

VOLUME – the amount of space taken up by a material. The volume of a block of wood is found by measuring its length, width, and height and multiplying the measurements together.

INDEX